DIARY OF A DRUG ADDICT

First English Edition
© Copyright 2009 by
United States Spiritist Council
www.spiritist.us

First published in Portuguese in 1995 by
Lichtverlag (www.lichtverlag.ch), under the
title *Diario de um Drogado*.

English Version Translation: Frederico Gouveia
English Version Translation Revision: Donald Gray-Raus
Electronic Edition: Edith Burkhard
Cover Design: Vivianne G. Thomsen

The English language version of this book is published and
distributed worldwide by the United States Spiritist Council.

Printed in the United States of America

TABLE OF CONTENTS:

DIARY OF A DRUG ADDICT

THE STORY OF THE SPIRIT

ANDRÉ K.

CHANNELED BY THE

MEDIUM

GORETE NEWTON

FOREWORD

This book tells the story of the spirit Andre K. who in 1995 was given permission to dictate his own story, after undergoing years of recovery treatment in the spirit realm, which included witnessing a weekly séance meeting held by a group of incarnate mediums. In this group, through the medium Gorete Newton, he describes his tragic death by drug overdose, which took place in 1977, while he lived in Zurich, Switzerland. It is a richly descriptive narrative for parents, their children and society, offering a glimpse of the afterlife consequences resulting from drug consumption. We hope you, the reader, enjoy it!

Much Peace,

Lichtverlag, Winterthur, Switzerland

INTRODUCTION

DIARY OF A DRUG ADDICT

THE ACCOUNTS OF A DRUG ADDICT

FROM HERE AND HEREAFTER

This is a compelling story of an adolescent who because of lack of care and affection in his home became an easy prey to the ill influence of drug users.

The other side reveals the gruesome side effects of drug usage as well as the ordeal drug addicts endure after their physical death.

It is a crucial reminder to all parents about the importance of the family institution and their role in guiding the spirits that were brought to them as their sons and daughters. Although it is a sad story it shows the aspect of constant renewal and the grandiosity of the divine laws that enable us to return and gather together again with our loved ones and make amends.

In its simplicity, the spirit Andre K. gives his testimony in a language that can be understood by adolescents and adults alike. This book should be read by every adolescent and every parent. Only by working together, with love and respect can parents and children guarantee a healthy and enlightened coexistence.

Jussara Korngold

Founder and President of the

Spiritist Group of New York

and the Spiritist Alliance for Books

PREFACE

To the indifferent or idle traveler, it is important to remember that we are all children of the purest love and light that exists in the Universe.

The impermanence of noble feelings and ideals inside of us is but a reflection of the current evolutionary and constructive state which we are all internally experiencing.

The seeds that lie dormant in our core await the liberating and cleansing opportunities to grow and offer service. Through our efforts and proactive attitude towards the greater Good, these seeds will blossom.

God always sends assistance and guidance when we are striving to remove the chains that hold us back in the evolutionary journey.

Let us do our part then.

The story presented here does not pretend to cast

an innovative light in humanity's discernment between good and evil. It simply shows our dear reader that love is readily available to assist everyone, at all times, offering infinite opportunities for us to review, ponder and start over. By benefiting from the lessons reaped in the past and present, we learn to grow, evolve and love, by loving.

We have what we deserve and we are what we think.

While we dwell in the muddy swamps of mental fatigue, one day a lily shall spring forth with strength and enthusiasm.

We still experience strong inner conflicts due to the abuses that have been collectively sown for thousands of years, with roots deeply stored in the human psyche. These conflicts are naturally aggravated by the adverse socioeconomic situation and problems in our world. As a result, we struggle to overcome the obstacles of our journey. But remember that the sole purpose of such trials is for us to triumph over them.

To the parents who are wondering how to best deal with their children, this story will help them realize how glorious their mission is in guiding those who, through them, come to the school of life once again.

The love in a family can be the most powerful tool available on Earth to connect souls and hearts with previous commitments to one another; it opens our eyes to subtleties in behaviors we notice in our loved ones. By noticing and being sensitive to them, we live more peacefully and in harmony under the same roof. This family love is capable of preventing and sometimes eliminating the roots of many pains and sorrows that manifest sooner or later in life.

To the young people of the world: if you are experiencing depression and melancholy, know that by watching your thoughts and emotions, you will determine your future. We are the fruits of our thoughts.

It's natural to experience uneasiness and restlessness when we feel the need to make changes in our lives. However, if we disarm ourselves of the powerful resources of optimism and hope, we risk falling in tragic ideas of suicide, especially in moments of trials and tests, which we sometimes don't anticipate.

We sincerely hope that these pages bring light to individuals experiencing addictions. May this story help parents and their children disentangle themselves from such problems, which are so common in our modern society.

Help each other out while there is time! By doing that, and by truly understanding, forgiving and serving one another, we can build our strengths together. And with this foundation, rest assured, you are investing in peace and victory, which will yield true happiness as you manifest the Glory of the Heavens on Earth!

May Jesus bless us all!

Marcelo J. Costa Netto

October 29, 2006

CHAPTER 1

MY REBIRTH

I was ready to return to life on Earth when I saw my future parents contemplating their various possibilities. "Do you think we should have a baby?" or "Wouldn't that compromise our careers?" or "Our expenses will increase should that happen." Everyday they pondered their options, went through this routine of arguments and discussions and yet, it seemed they were not able to ever decide and make up their minds. At that time, some of my spirit friends who were constantly inspiring my intended parents with thoughts of having a child accompanied me on my journey to be born. Finally, one day, they came to a decision and accepted to bring me into this world.

Overwhelmed by the excitement of their decision, my parents began to buy everything they could think of to prepare for their future baby: sets of small clothes, cradle, toys, countless other gifts, all to make me feel welcome. I for one was immensely happy to be born into their lives and live with them.

The time of my birth came and at first they looked at their newborn with great affection giving me all the care in the world. But after a few sleepless nights, when I cried all through it because of the colic, they would get irritated and angry. They had no idea how much pain I felt and it also hurt me to see my parents upset with me. This of course also meant that as they got angrier, my colic would get worse.

After a while I was crying less, but I was not seeing them very often either. A strange woman took care of me. I didn't know who she was, but I have to say that I was always clean and seemed happy, ready to greet my parents when they got home. What a joy it was, to feel their arms around me and to see their smiling faces as they looked at me!

CHAPTER 2

EARLY CHILDHOOD

After a while I began to walk and toddled towards my mother's arms babbling my first words: "Mummy, Mummy!" and at other times it would be my father who caught my attention. I would stumble towards him shouting: "Daddy, Daddy".

A little later, I began to eat by myself and of course accidents happened in the beginning. My parents would get irritated again: "What a mess! This boy spills everything everywhere!" During those moments, when I'd see my mother so angry I would tell myself: "I'm going to learn everything really fast so that she will be happy with me and thankful for having had me." Still, instead of becoming easier with my childish ways, their dissatisfaction only grew worse.

"This year we won't be able to take a vacation; the money is too short" my father would say.

"I know", echoed my mother: "We haven't been

able to do anything since his birth".

"I agree, but remember, you were the one who wanted a child. I told you the time wasn't right", my fahter would say.

In no time my parents would start arguing and fighting because of me. I loved them very much and decided that, once I was all grown up, I would work very hard to give them all the vacations they had missed because of me.

Time went by; I grew older and began to attend school. During my first years in kindergarten, whenever I was just a little late to the dinner table, I would hear harsh complaints and accusations from my parents, words that really hurt. "We do everything for you and in return all you give us is more headaches and more bills! Because of you our life has become unbearable! I can't even work anymore because I have to take care of you! Here's your plate, now eat it!" mother would say impatiently.

CHAPTER 3

PUBERTY

I felt very confused and guilty; was I really that much of a problem? Was I getting in the way to the point of ruining their lives? How could I do this to them when I loved them so much? I began to think of myself as a total failure. My soul was beginning to fill up with sadness and there were moments when I just wanted to die, so as to put an end to everyone's 'headaches'. I did my homework with enormous difficulty and my progress in school deteriorated. I didn't sleep well. I kept thinking how it was possible that a person could be so worthless. Things went quickly from bad to worse and I was unable to concentrate at all in school. My parents thought that their many sacrifices had been in vain and their attitude towards me changed. The mixture of anger and frustration they felt increased and they slowly turned from yelling, to cursing and finally spanking me, sometimes for small things.

CHAPTER 4

ADOLESCENCE

The years passed and I entered my adolescence. In growing from a child to a young man I began to alter the way I thought. My feelings towards my parents began to change and I started feeling anger and resentment. By the age of 14 I was answering them back in the same way that they talked to me. The fighting and arguing became an everyday occurrence at home. It was during those times that I would seek peace and quiet by going out and walking on the streets near my house. On one of those nights I saw a guy I knew from school. He always looked a little strange to me, with the way he dressed and his spiked hair which set him apart. He was very quiet, rarely talked to anyone, and was always alone at school. When he saw me walking on the street, I said "hi" and asked him:

"What are you doing out here"?

"I'm going to meet my friends and get my *shine*"; he said, with a grin.

"What do you mean?"

"Man, you're really stupid, aren't you?"

I flushed with embarrassment. I didn't understand what he had meant. Disguising my confusion, I said:

"Okay man, go for it, it's cool..."

"It's more than cool, it's *HAPPINESS*!"

What was that about? I thought for a minute; *Happiness*. The word rang painfully in my mind. I wanted to be happy more than anything. Why didn't anyone teach us to be happy? I came back home late that night, not knowing what to expect. I knew that my parents were going to argue and complain, but I wasn't prepared for what I was about to hear:

"You're home, finally! As of tomorrow, you're to cook your own food and start assuming some responsibilities around here! After all, you're old enough to take care of yourself. In fact, I'm going to start working again, to see if our life improves. I'm sick and tired of taking care of you for nothing!"

Hearing my mother talk like that, I felt numb, and was actually surprised at my own reaction, since I felt utterly indifferent to what she had just said. She could say whatever she wanted to say. I didn't care anymore. I was about to enter into a new phase in my life; a phase where I would be completely on my own.

As I dictate my story, now being out of my body and still receiving treatment, I have a much better understanding of the relationship problems I had with my parents. I'm conscious of the fact that we are all God's children although only a few actually are aware of that or care about this while in the physical body. Yet, we all need to have faith and hope for better days. We need reassurance so that we don't suffer miserably, thinking that our problems are the biggest ones in the world. As for parenthood in general, what a challenging mission! My parents were supposed to love me despite my flaws and were not to give in to their feelings of impatience, anger and frustration. They should have helped me along the way by showing me brighter paths, solutions and correcting my flaws with love and care. Had it been so we could have shared the happiness of being together up to this day. Had my parents used the tools of love, patience and understanding while helping me when I was little, things would have turned out much differently. Their failings were weaknesses of their spirit. As a matter of fact, they had been my children in a previous lifetime and I for one had not been a compassionate or understanding father either. I had simply given them all the material things they needed without correcting their mistakes or guiding them through their difficult moments. Now it had been my turn to serve as an instrument for the development of their nobler feelings of compassion, understanding and care. Unfortunately, we all failed!

CHAPTER 5

THE TRAP

The days and months went by. In the mornings I would eat anything I found in our kitchen and go to school. I was often late to class, absent-minded and didn't actively participate in any of my classes. As a result, I was sent to see the school psychologist who in turn contacted my parents. They were outraged by my behaviour. How could I explain this feeling of emptiness I felt in my soul, these thoughts of hopelessness and low self-esteem?

One day I remembered the guy with the spiked haircut and strange clothes who was always alone at school. Maybe he was going through the same problems. I remembered the day when I had met him on the street and he had told me about happiness. I saw him at recess and decided to approach him, in the hopes of learning more about this happiness.

"Hey Weber, how are you?"

"Ok man, you?"

"Very bad, my life sucks!"

"Of course life sucks. We are born and then wait for death, it doesn't make sense; it's ridiculous. There are only a few emotions worth having and the rest is just problems. Humanity is worthless; I don't understand this joke of being born only to have to die afterwards. That is the reason why I live in the moment, in this hour and don't waste time thinking of others or the "bigger picture" that they sometimes refer to. I don't care what these idiots think, these puppets of society. I am my own man and everybody else can just go to hell!"

"I know man" I replied. "I think I agree with you. I still don't understand the whole reason for life. What's it all about? What is the purpose of a father, a mother? How about school? People behave like robots, doing the same things day in and day out. Who or what are they trying to please? I am so fed up; I wish I could just disappear..."

"You need to stop being such an idiot trying to look, talk and act like these robots of society."

"But how if there are no other ways?" I asked.

"Look, I come to school just so I don't lose the right to get certain things, but my life is elsewhere. I have my own friends and they are my true friends. We all hang out and do everything together. We enjoy the high of disconnecting from this crappy world so we can savour the 'shiny' side of life!"

"But Weber, you are talking about drugs, right?"

"No man, I'm talking about wonders. *This* life is a

drug!"

"But drugs are bad for you, they destroy people!"

"Whoa, man, look at me! Hello! I'm alive! Am I talking to you now or am I dead? No, I am very much alive. This whole idea about drugs being bad for you, don't believe it. It's just society talking because they are not collecting taxes from the people selling them. That's why they give drugs a bad reputation. Why don't they ban alcohol or smoking? Cigarettes are out there in the market, aren't they? You can buy cigarettes anywhere, anytime, right? These corporations make me sick! You think they don't make any money? I tell you, they make millions! How do you think the 'shine' and the smoke come into the country? All they have to do is buy a few customs officers and everything gets cleared through. The dealers disguise their stuff and get it in with their regular products; everything works out fine.

"I'd never have imagined that."

"That's because these corporate guys and the people in power don't want the masses to think things through. They want to do the thinking for them".

As I listened to Weber, I was convinced that he was right. I began to look at our society in a new way, considering it corrupt and the root cause of all the evils in our world. Weber had introduced me to a certain way of thinking, one in which humans belonged to a decadent biological species, one where individuals were born, grew up and died without a purpose or any reason whatsoever.

Now that I find myself in the spiritual realm, where

kind and friendly spirits assist me in the detoxification process – though many years have already gone by, I am still impregnated with the toxins of the substances I consumed – I see how clouded all our thoughts are when we are living in the physical world. While on earth, we are not taught to be rationally aware of, or understand something that is greater than ourselves, outside our material reality. There are many paths, thoroughly explained by the various religions, all of which are very useful and serve to protect humans against the traps and seductions that the physical journey presents. However, the two biggest evils, Selfishness and Pride, sometimes blind even the souls who are on a religious and elevated path of self-discovery. Through the wide doors of Selfishness and Pride, our astute enemies can easily catch us. The youth of the world, including myself, for the most part, remains vulnerable to the negative impressions that are emanated by our brothers in the spiritual world, who still dwell in the shadows. They try imprinting negative ideas and images about religion in our minds. As a result, many teenagers and young adults consider religion a waste of time, of no use or any help whatsoever. We then begin to steer away from a path that would have protected and given us moral defenses against the traps that may ultimately lead to tragedy; traps that first appear in our lives during the crucial years of adolescence. When parents begin teaching their children that God exists, that Jesus came to the world for humans to be happy; when they teach their children to develop their faith from an early age, a rational and conscious faith; that the need and merit of an individual determines the outcome of his or her prayers; when all of this is passed on to children, they will then be able to transition through their ado-

lescence more confident, resolved, stronger; and the world will certainly become a better place.

CHAPTER 6

PLUNGING INTO ILLUSION

I was impressed after the exchange I had with Weber. He was very intelligent. What a strong personality! He knew about things. I began to spend more and more time with him and after a few days I was having my first cigarette. I held it between my fingers with pride, feeling confident about myself. This was 1975, when I lived in Zurich, Switzerland. A couple of months went by, and I was introduced to Weber's group of friends. The first time I hung out with them, they made me participate in a sort of ritual; we sat in a circle with a straw; it was filled with the so-called shiny powder (cocaine) and we had to press a finger against the bottom of the straw, while inhaling from the other end. We would then lick our finger and pass the straw to the next person. I was last and had to inhale whatever was left. I was very scared. Deep inside, a strong voice was telling me: "Get out of here! Leave now! Be strong!" I suddenly felt an urge to get up and run out of there. But since I sat there for a while, not knowing what to do, the other guys in the circle began to yell and make fun of me:

"What's up man, you're gonna chicken out?"

"What's it gonna be? You're gonna go for it or not?"

"Are you scared? It's just a powder! Let's go!"

"Is mom's powder less scary? Hahahahaha"!

Between that inner voice urging me to leave and Weber's friends sitting in the circle making fun of me, I gave in, not listening to the voice of my spirit guide, who was trying everything to get me out of there. So, under the pressure of Weber's friends, I brought the straw to my nose and, almost panicking, inhaled the rest of the powder. I said:

"I don't feel anything"

"Of course you don't. Breathe in deep, with all your strength!"

So I did that and finished the powder inside the straw. I immediately felt dizzy. My body was tingling and I was no longer myself. I felt happy; I was smiling, euphoric and also kind of lethargic. A multitude of sensations took over my body. I heard my friends laughing hysterically at all the faces I was making.

CHAPTER 7

CONSEQUENCES

In less than a month I gradually began to look more and more like Weber. I changed my habits; stopped cutting my hair, rejected society with its costumes and conventions, and began looking at the other kids my age with pity and disdain. I would go out every night with Weber and by the time my parents got home, I was already out. At first they kept asking me where I went and there were fights and arguments on a daily basis. Nonetheless, I kept getting home later and later. My parents slowly stopped stressing about my behaviour. They were filled with disillusionment and felt it was hopeless to argue or discuss my actions any further. So, they disconnected completely from me.

The months went by and my friends began asking me for money to pay for the powder. After all, they were paying for everything and only giving me what was left in the straw to inhale. But how could I afford it if I had no money and no job?

They told me to take small amounts of cash from

my father's wallet and my mother's purse. I did this on alternate days, so as not to raise any suspicions. By the end of the month, I had enough money to buy the shine. Naturally this sequence of pick pocketing did not go unnoticed by my parents; they knew something was wrong. They asked each other if one took money from the other. Only after a while did they start suspecting me, and decided to set a trap. While I was out one night, they counted all their money and wrote down the amount on a piece of paper. Then, they put the purse and wallet in the usual place and waited for me to come home. When I arrived, I went to my dad's wallet and was caught in the act. It was almost 2:00am. They turned on all the lights in the house and came to my room.

"You are a thief!" My father glared at me with his eyes and I could hear in his voice how much he despised me. I just stared at them blankly; my movements were slow and emotionless. I didn't care, I just sat on my bed, not answering or reacting to any of their questions and accusations. Only then did my parents realize that there was something really wrong with me, and yet they could not figure out what. My dad began to threaten me, saying that if I ever took anything from their wallets again, they would take me to the police.

"What do you do with the money you steal from us anyway?" – he asked.

"I have been going out with my girlfriend."

"Poor girl! Who is she? Where does she live? We need to let her parents know that she is in really bad company! She is dating a thief!"

I felt so insulted and hurt that I screamed, from the depths of my soul and began to weep uncontrollably. I exploded at them, yelling:

"You are monsters! Get out of my room! I hate you!"

My mother began to cry as if something inside of her stirred and was suddenly awakened. My father told me to shut up, and said:

"That is the reward we get for raising a child with so much love and care, making sure he always had everything he needed!"

I laughed hysterically and replied:

"Indeed I have everything. Ever since I was born, I never went hungry or cold, but when it came to 'love' and 'care', these came nowhere near me. You only love yourselves and the damn money!"

A huge fight broke out after what I said. My dad jumped on me and we rolled on the floor, punching each other, while my mom tried to separate us. Since she couldn't match our strengths, she ran to the neighbours' house to get help and they called the police.

We were finally separated and taken to a room to talk. After the neighbours realized that it was a "father and son" incident and not a burglary, they were more relieved. My dad, not wanting to tell anyone the reason for the fight, said it was a situation that could happen in any family, to which the police officer responded:

"I just hope it never happens in mine...."

After that day, total indifference emerged between the three of us at home. Our family life disintegrated completely. Although we lived in the same house, we never exchanged words again. When my parents decided to take a vacation, my mom came into my room and told me: "We're going on a trip. Here's everything you need and some extra money in case of an emergency."

CHAPTER 8

THE ABYSS

They left and I was relieved to have the house for myself. I invited my friends over and we had a party, where I was again put through the ritual, only this time with a syringe. We all sat in our usual circle and with only one syringe, each one injected a bit of the white liquid in the vein. I was no longer afraid of the substance. I had become another person, indifferent and empty, numb to any feelings. I only cared about the present moment.

The following day I woke up trembling, feeling very cold and weak. I got up, ate something, but my trembling didn't stop. I drank a bit of whisky, which made me feel better. My body was debilitated. I would eat very little and party all night. During my parents' month-long vacation, I enjoyed what I considered to be freedom. I went to many gatherings, in which its sole purpose was to take drugs. The fact of the matter was that we were all lacking guidance, love, patience and conscientiousness from our surroundings. I became totally alienated, trying to experience as many sensations as I could and within as little time as possible. I would artificially enhance my emotions with these drugs while cultivating a sick friendship with the other kids around me, all of us heading for the same tragic end. I had some purple spots on my arms, due to my inexperience with the syringes; many times I injected the liquid in my skin. I began applying the syringes on my legs in order to hide the purple spots and avoid my friends making fun of me. The conversations between us were dismal. Most of the time there was almost no dialogue. We would speak meaningless words, without context or any sequential logic.

Each morning my trembling got worse and the only thing to carry me over until the next injection was the whisky. All the money was gone and so was the food. I began selling some objects from my room to those individuals that take advantage of the miserable conditions of an addict in desperate need. It had been a year since I first started inhaling and 20 days into the syringe routine. I needed the drug everyday just to keep me going.

CHAPTER 9

DESPERATION

I was getting desperate at the idea of my parents coming home soon. The house was a total mess. I didn't want to see them again, because I knew they were going to flip when they saw the house. I would console myself by thinking:

"If I clean everything up, they won't notice anything." I would look at all that mess and just could not find the strength to do anything about it. It was as if a powerful energy absorbed every positive impulse I had, leaving me in a sick state of inertia. Only later would I fully understand what was happening to me.

In two days my parents would be coming back home. I had moments of uncontrollable emotions, alternated with total apathy and indifference to everything. Sometimes I cried desperately like a child, because deep down in my heart I loved them and felt like I was the worst creature in the world.

On the night before their arrival, I went to meet my

friends in the usual place, a square in the town where we used to gather. This square, called the *'Platzspitz'*, was the meeting place of all the drug addicts in Zurich*; it was very sad. That day we used one big syringe that should have been enough for all of us. One of the girls in the circle though, when it was her turn, took the syringe and injected all of the liquid in her vein. One of the kids screamed: "Why did you do this Regula!?" He jumped on her, trying desperately to suck the liquid out from her vein but it was too late. At first, the girl laughed hysterically, and then began to cry, shiver and shake violently. What happened next was unbelievable. She fell on the floor and began hitting herself, scratching her arms, legs, grabbing her hair, screaming and going into severe shock. We all got scared and one of us said: "Let's get out of here, before they blame us for this!"

We all ran away from the square, afraid of being caught and accused in case she died. At the time, I happened to be holding all of the powder we were going to consume that night. I rushed back home with four envelopes, enough to fill eight big syringes after diluting it in water. As soon as I got home I went straight to the living room. I was nervous and needed to calm down. I hadn't yet injected myself that evening and didn't have a syringe on me. I inhaled some of the powder, feeling very rich for having that amount of drugs just for myself.

Needlepark – Gathering place for drug addicts, notorious during the 1970's and 80's. The area was officially closed off in 1992 by the Zurich Police Department and cleaned up. Reopened in 1993, it has since become a safe public park.

(Translators' note)

I knew that this feeling would end the next morning. My parents would be back and my peace and freedom were in jeopardy.

I went back to the square to get a syringe and saw an ambulance taking a body away, which I assumed was Regula's. I wondered if she had really died. When that thought came to my mind, I imagined my own death and asked myself what it must be like when you die; when you end it all and get rid of all the problems... Who knows, even my parents might suffer, feeling regret for all those years of indifference? As this idea became stronger in my head, I began seeing them come home from their trip, crying desperately over my dead body, screaming:

"Our little child, what did we do? Oh God, he's dead!"

Wow, that would really be painful to them! I wouldn't exist any longer, it would all be over and I would finally get some rest. But then I thought: what about Heaven? Did it really exist? What about Hell? No, all nonsense, I thought. Those were nothing but fantasies made up to scare and control the masses.

I found a syringe at the 'Platzspitz' and took it home to wash. I then mixed all the powder with water and sugar, stirred and filled the syringe to the top with the mixture. There was bit of whisky left in the bottle, which I finished in one big gulp. I injected a little bit of the liquid into my vein and soon began to feel relaxed and calm.

It was very late at night when I began to look back over my life. All the negative images I had in my mind, all the suffering I went through were associated with my parents. The house was a mess and I didn't feel like cleaning it up. I just didn't have the energy or the willpower to do it. I was in an absolute state of numbness. While my parents were away, I felt free and in control, but now, as they were soon coming home, my freedom was going to end and the fighting and arguing would resume. I was not going to tolerate that any longer! I was suddenly afraid and just wanted to run away from home and live on the streets. I thought about the cold and quickly reasoned that I wouldn't survive for too long. That's when I decided to die at home. That way I would end this nightmare and inflict tremendous pain on my parents! They would finally feel in their own flesh the pain they had caused me during all these years. Something or someone was telling me to go for it:

"Hurry up already... don't you chicken out this time!"

I took the remaining powder in the packets and inhaled them, but there was very little left. I went to my room and thought about writing a letter to my parents. While sitting down with the pen and paper I began noticing my feelings towards them. I loved and hated them at the same time. I thought I was a huge burden in their lives. I did not feel loved by them but felt more like a burden to them.

I sat on my bed, determined to end my life, once and for all. I took the big syringe, which was filled with the mixture I had made earlier, and injected all of the liquid into my vein. I was careful to use a thick needle so as to avoid clogging. What if that wasn't enough? That's okay I thought, I would find a way to disappear, no matter what. As soon as I finished the injection, I felt my heart beating faster and more irregularly. I felt a strange sensation; I couldn't really tell if it was cold or hot. My heart kept beating faster and I felt a sharp pain in my chest. That's when I started to convulse and my body began to twitch and shake violently. Everything seemed surreal. It was like I was fighting the furniture in my room, as I rolled on the floor, hitting myself and bumping into the objects around me. The chest pain suddenly became unbearable and I began hearing voices, laughter and screaming. They were desperately screaming at me:

"Give me a little bit of what's left in the syringe!

Just a little bit! Give it to me!"

"Hey man, where's our powder? Give it back, now!"

"We want it! Come on get closer, we want to feel the high too! Get closer!"

My head was spinning and I felt nauseous, my stomach was empty and felt very cold. I was debilitated from the excessive drinking and the drugs during the last month. As soon as all the shaking and trembling stopped, I crawled under my desk in the corner of my room and just sat there, resting my arms and head between my knees, not wanting to look up at those shadowy figures screaming at me. I wanted to go to sleep, but I felt like I was in a nightmare with noises, talking, agitation and laughter all around me. I kept my head down, not wanting to face anyone or anything. The funny thing was that whenever I closed my eyes I still had a clear image of all that was going on. I suddenly felt extremely cold. I hadn't yet realized that I was out of my physical body; that was gone; I had killed it but didn't want to admit that I was physically dead. Like a fetus out of the uterus, I was seeking warmth. I was trembling and shaking with that overwhelming sensation of cold, as I hid under my desk. The hours went by, it was broad daylight and those creatures still roamed in my room, all around me, asking the same thing:

"Just a little bit more of the drug, c'mon!"

After a while I heard a different kind of scream. It was my mother: "Oh my God! What happened? Our son is lying on the floor!" When I saw her, I realized I was dead, that is, my body was lifeless on the floor, next to my bed. She was in a state of panic; I could see the pain on her face and the desperate suffering she was feeling. My dad walked into the room, got close to the body and realized what had happened. After a glancing around the room, he calmly concluded:

"Just as I suspected; his problem was drugs. I'm going to go call the police."

I couldn't believe what I was hearing. I was in shock. Who was that man? How could he feel absolutely no pain for the death of his son? Was he just waiting for this to happen?

I died in 1977. Until 1994, I experienced all the horrors that most suicides go through, inside my own home. Thanks to kind and loving friends, who rescued me from this nightmare I am able today to think of my parents with more compassion. They were under my care in the past as my children, and because of my in-

difference, I ended up nurturing selfishness, conceit, pride and apathy in them towards me. I was reaping what I had once sown in their hearts.

The police was quick to arrive at the scene and take my body away while my mother was crying. As I saw the scene unfold, I got sad and very depressed. As for my dad, it seemed that his problems were over with my departure. To make matters worse, these horrible creatures - which I learned later were people just like me that had followed a similar path and ended up in the same situation as I was right now - kept constantly tormenting me. They wouldn't leave me alone! I wanted to calm myself down, relax and sleep. Still, I experienced the urge for the drug and it was driving me insane. This yearning did not go away with my body. In fact, it felt more real and stronger now than ever before. I would jump desperately in front of my parents, begging them for something to inject myself with. Naturally, they couldn't hear or see me. After trying everything to get their attention and not able to satisfy my urge, I had an idea: maybe if I went to the Platzspitz where I used to meet my friends, I'd find a way to use the drug. So I left the house. But I was not prepared for what I was about to witness there. It was a scene out of a horror movie. In this town square, I observed hundreds of discarnate people huddling closely, as they tried to absorb the emanations from the bodies of the kids who were in the square injecting drugs. I was desperate and started to do the same. I would get close to someone who was about to inhale or inject the drug and 'breathe in' all that emanated from the person's body through their pores. It was a way of capturing their intoxicated energies and this gave me some relief. I found myself with hundreds of other creatures, consum-

47

ing drugs through those that were still alive. I felt like a vampire, straight out of a horror movie.

Many months went by and I got used to this new way of life, sucking the emanations of people's bodies to calm my urges. I would go back and forth between my house and this disgraceful square to meet the young people who gathered around this fantasy, this terrible illusion, totally unaware that they were being followed by dozens of perverse creatures. These creatures, who all went down the same tortuous path I had recently gone. They celebrated every time they were able to convince a new young boy or girl to try out the drug for the first time and proceeded to lure them to the square to meet the others. These poor youngsters came mostly from homes where compassion, warmth and understanding were scarce. So they sought company here, maybe some friendship, even if it was destructive, which they knew deep down to be the case. The drug addicts showed this deceptive care for one another, almost a bit of compassion and understanding, because they all suffered from the same thing; lack of love. Many of them had reincarnated into the homes of former enemies from past lives and lacked the strength, faith, hope and abnegation to accept and withstand the corrective trials that God had prepared for them as an educational tool for progress. These kids became victims of their own debts, incurred in previous existences.

Somehow, there was solidarity and understanding amongst the kids in the square, as they enjoyed being with one another. They all suffered deeply the loss of one of their friends, whenever one died and went on to what we thought was 'nothingness'. Yet there I was, more alive than ever and more harmful to others than ever before. We roamed the streets of that town day and night. We tried, like parasites to cling to an addict's body and the scene was literally infernal. If someone in the physical world could see what I was seeing, they would conclude that sheer Darkness ruled that square, even in broad daylight.

CHAPTER 10

THE RESCUE

Sometimes, there would be different movements in the Platzspitz, and my friends - they had become my friends after a while - would desperately run away and hide. This happened many times and it took me a while to discover exactly why. Since I didn't know what was happening, I would run away too and hide along with my friends. Until one day I said to myself that I was going to get to the bottom of this and find out what made them all so scared that they'd always run away. One day we were, as usual, packed around a circle of kids trying to suck as much of their intoxicated energies as we could, when suddenly I saw all my discarnate friends running for their lives: "It's 'them'! Let's get out of here!" But I stayed behind and noticed some beings dressed like police officers, nurses and doctors arrive in what I assumed looked like ambulances. What made my friends run for their lives was the light that shined from these visitors. We were all aware of the bad things we were doing, in our constant efforts to lure young kids to the square to try out drugs for the first time and get them hooked. We feared being arrested as criminals. In fact, I saw some of my friends being captured by glowing ropes, which seemed to have a calming effect since their faces suddenly relaxed and, while yawning, they would close their eyes and fall asleep. These visitors would leave the square just as quickly as they arrived. After a while, very few who were taken would eventually come back to the square; most were never seen again. I was trying to figure out where they were being taken. Were they being examined? Were these doctors conducting experiments on them? I waited and wondered until one day, while at the Platzspitz, I saw an old man who had recently been taken away. Since the people who eventually came back usually looked much older and were always furious and even frightening, I was very cautious to approach him. I finally took the courage, walked over and asked:

"Hey, what happened to you when you were taken away by the 'Police'? What happened to the others? Why didn't they come back?"

I was so anxious to find out the answers that I asked many questions at once.

"These guys are morons! Idiots! They fell for the puny talk of a half dozen fanatics, these religious lunatics. I have no idea where they went!"

"But who are these shiny-looking visitors that come here? They have this light that glows around them."

"Forget about that man! We've got the real shine! Let's go get some more of that shiny powder...

These 'glowing' visitors are always getting in the

way of our group; they put crazy ideas in our heads and try to convince us to get out of here! They always screw things up for us! But, oh no! Not me! I don't fall for their stories..."

CHAPTER 11

FIRST CONTACT WITH ENLIGHTENED SPIRITS

I kept thinking though, trying to find a reasonable explanation for all of this. I made an effort to imagine how other places looked like and where these people came from. Why did we all look like shadows? Why did these visitors have this light shining around them as if it came from inside of their bodies? A new thought crept in my mind right there and then: I wanted to see how a trip with them would be like. Where would I be taken? After all, if I didn't like it, I was apparently free to come back as I had seen it happen with some of the others. I made up my mind; 'next time they come to the square, I'll let them capture me', I thought. And so, when I saw them coming, I stayed as close to them as my courage allowed, and to my astonishment, they didn't capture me. Instead, they got close to me and looked into my eyes with great kindness and affection. In peaceful and pleasant voices they told me that if I wished to accompany them, they would be more than happy to have me. It had been so long since I felt such kind, loving and caring feelings. I was totally unprepared by their unexpected attitude towards me. I asked foolishly:

"Aren't you going to tie me up?"

One of them answered calmly, with a smile:

"If you wish to come by your own desire, why would we need to tie you up? All people who are willing to change for the Good on their own accord don't need the chains of correction".

My heart started to beat faster. I was scared of the unknown and hopeful at the same time. I climbed into the vehicle and off we went. I enjoyed the silence inside, something I had not been able to find for decades. It seems unbelievable, but ever since the moment I had left my physical body, this was the first time I was experiencing silence. I felt such peace and tranquillity.

I enjoyed every moment of it as much as I could. As I sat there, I thought:

"How can this be? We are dead! The so-called 'hell' that all of us have heard so much about, was right here on earth! What were these people doing? Who were they and where were they taking us?"

Suddenly an older gentleman, who was sitting in front of me, with a pleasant light around his face, told me:

"My son, we build our own hell by the wrong paths we choose to follow while on Earth. We entangle ourselves in confusion and end up attracting negative situations and circumstances, which lead to emotional instability. Before we know it, if we're not strong enough, we fall into a bottomless pit. Hell is merely an expression of the pains we all feel. These pains are the result of misusing our free will, one of the greatest gifts granted to us by God. When we choose to remain ignorant and lazy, not actively seeking to enlighten our soul, we get stuck and slowly begin to sink into swamps of illusions. As for us, we're assistants sent here by divine mercy, since God never abandons any of His children. He grants us all countless opportunities to renew ourselves until we're convinced of the practical usefulness of Love. It is only through Love that we relieve the burdens of the multitude of sins that still oppress us at our given stage; and so we're slowly learning to always love and forgive, just as He always loves and forgives us".

I was perplexed because I had not opened my mouth at all. I had only asked these questions in my head. And yet this gentleman was talking to me and answering everything! He continued:

"For us, my son, thought has no boundaries. We work with Jesus for those who are suffering. We can hear the thoughts of all people that vibrate in our frequency or in lower ones without any problems. Naturally, this is not the case for everyone, as there are many spirits that still tune only to the thoughts of their fellow brothers and sisters who are on the same level as they are. This is the law of 'magnetic affinity'. It is true that 'bad hears bad and good hears good'. Evil is only able to reach and plot against good when good is not secure, confident, and thus becomes vulnerable to temptations. Since we have free will, each one of us can make decisions and choose the path that suits us best. While we are imprisoned in a physical body we are more vulnerable and exposed to influences, but it is always we, who ultimately determine our own lives. At the end, there are either more credits or more debits, according to our decisions."

I absorbed those words like someone who takes a pill for a deep pain. I told him how I understood his words:

"While we are in the physical body we are exposed to many temptations. Because we are ignorant of the realities of the spiritual life - the life that continues after the death of the physical body - we see very few options and we end up choosing badly".

He said:

"In part you're right, but one doesn't need to know that life goes on in order to choose wisely and follow the path of goodness. There are a great many who overcome their flaws just by listening to the voice of their conscience. That voice is always guiding and inspiring them to follow the path of good. The problem is that most of the time we don't listen to our conscience because it is going against our wishes and interests at the moment or because of our inferior instincts. If we make the effort to triumph over our flaws and negative instincts, we will progress spiritually. Do you remember the first time you tried the drug?"

"Yes", I said.

"Do you remember that sudden urge you felt to get up and run out of there?"

"Yes, I do remember that."

"Well, that was your guardian angel, your spirit guide who was trying everything to prevent you from taking that first step into the abyss you ultimately fell in. He did all he could, but the decision was yours. He has no right to force your muscles to run out of there, but he could and did inspire in you a vigorous urge to put the drug down and to get out. Because we all have free will, you made the decision and tuned your thoughts to a frequency that darkness vibrates in. You fell, like a defenseless victim, into their trap. And yet here you are, today, still free to decide on whatever path you choose to take."

Although my mind was opening up to new ideas and possibilities, I suddenly became very anxious and started to cry. I turned to the kind gentleman and begged him:

"Please help me sir! I can't take this anymore! I need to absorb some energy so I can calm down! I need the drug! I know that I'm addicted to it and it eats me alive! Please, help me!"

I began to tremble and convulse. I was desperate for the drug. The vehicle stopped and the man took me by the arms like a father carrying a handicapped son. I was no longer able to see what was happening around me. I was in a daze. I begged this man for some compassion and he held me in his arms like a merciful father, looking at me with penetrating eyes. He placed me onto what looked like a hospital bed and like an attentive doctor who is touched by his patient's suffering, he said to me:

"Don't you worry, you will get better soon".

"You already took the first step towards recovery. You have shown willingness to change, to want to be happy. Now surrender yourself and trust in Jesus. I need you to sleep now. We've just arrived from a very long journey."

With my head still trembling and my whole body shivering, I nodded. He then placed his hand on my forehead and induced me into a deep sleep.

CHAPTER 12

IN THE HOSPITAL

When I woke up I was in a huge room with subdued lighting. As soon as I opened my eyes, an old lady, who looked like a nurse, approached my bed and asked:

"How are you my child? Feeling better?" "I don't know" I answered. "I am tired and dizzy. I feel nauseous... I think I'm going to vomit".

She was obviously prepared for this and immediately placed a large receptacle in front of me. I was astonished at what I saw coming out of my stomach. I vomited huge pieces of compact dark matter. It looked like organs, kidneys and thick, coagulated tissue material. It was terrifying!

The sweet lady held the container with one hand and caressed my head with the other, telling me in a sweet voice, like a mother talking to a son:

"Don't panic. It's okay. Don't get scared. Trust and thank Jesus. These are residues of the substances that were harming your body. They were lacerating your insides."

I was puzzled at her explanation. How could I still have a body, if I had already "died"? It only took the thought for her to look at me, and answer:

"When the physical body dies, the spiritual body remains. We are eternal beings and our conscience sometimes is awakened only through pain; we are all individuals in the treatment of a long evolutionary journey."

I was taken to an area I had never seen before. There, a procession of beautiful spirits, dressed in simple tunics made from a material that radiated a soothing energy, came down a large staircase. Murals decorated the walls surrounding us, displaying paintings and poems by artists who were inspired by Love. Our guardian angels and spirit guides, who looked just as bright and beautiful, held hands and formed an outer circle of protection around us. From them, lights of different colours and nuances emanated towards us, embracing and making us all feel incredibly calm. I wasn't able to understand what was happening exactly, since I still felt tired and nauseous.

The next impression I had was in a different room. There was a large table with incarnate people sitting around it. They were praying with their eyes closed. I noticed a tremendous difference in the kinds of energy coming from each one. Some of them were being pressured and bothered by spirits who were trying to distract them from the noble purposes of this meeting, which was to assist and rescue souls in need of help. The group was studying the life of Jesus with a book that looked like the Gospel. They were reading the passage in which the Pharisees confronted Jesus and he states that what belonged to Caesar should be given to Caesar.

After this study session ended, they closed their eyes and began praying. They were getting ready to start the second part of the meeting. Sick and desperate individuals, who were in urgent need of help, were placed behind some of the people that sat around the table. I was told to stand next to an old lady with short white hair. Under her influence I was able to hear and understand what the other mediums on the table were saying and how they were talking to the brothers and sisters that were in desperate need of help. They were being treated with immense kindness, respect and compassion. A powerful feeling of hope overwhelmed my senses and touched my heart. I wanted to change and I wanted that with all of my strength! I needed to understand and feel this love they were referring to and I wanted to get to know this merciful Christ, who forgives everyone. With the sweet old lady's help and the fusing of both of our energies together, I felt ready and confident to take the next step to improve my condition. I understood that only through my efforts and their help would I get well again.

Today, knowing our master Jesus a little better, I thank Him for his Love, protection and mercy. I also thank the mediums, who with goodwill and charity in their hearts dedicate sacred hours of their lives for this important ministry. They give hope and love to those who are lost and confused in the spiritual world.

Thanks to this kind lady, I was able to hear words of consolation and hope. I was in a state of bliss. If I could I would never have left that room! However, as the minutes went by, I was called back to my own reality. I was suddenly confronted with the irresistible urge for the drug again. I began to shiver and tremble. Like a child that wants to stay at a party a little longer, I began to cry. My eyes were searching for that compassionate older gentleman from the vehicle that had brought me to this sphere. Upon thinking that, I immediately saw him next to me and with the same fatherly care he held me by the arms, like a child without strength. He asked me with warmth and loving care:

"Do you want to go back to where you came from? Or would you rather stay here with us and begin a new life? We can help you in each step of the way".

"Please, for heaven's sake", I pleaded, in between my tears and shivers from my all-consuming addiction, "Please help me if you can!" The gentleman held me by the arms. Looking at me in a significant way, I could feel he was trying to inspire me to have courage and determination. New ideas started to flood my mind.

From that moment on I began a long journey back to recovery; a journey that required courage and acceptance of my situation. Whenever I felt insecure or doubted my own strengths, those illuminated brothers and sisters were right there for me, inspiring me, giving me courage and resolve. My detoxification treatment would take a while and I needed all the support I could get.

There were times during my recovery when I felt at the edge of an abyss, ready to abandon everything and run back to that awful town square. At times I felt like I was dying but then I would remember, that I was already 'dead'. I gradually became more convinced that it is best to confront your pain when it makes its presence felt, looking forward, with confidence and hopeful anticipation to better days ahead. This confidence and reassurance took hold sooner than I had thought.

My detoxification treatment in the spiritual world lasted the equivalent of 18 months in 'Earth time'. During this period, I was always taken to that meeting where the mediums gathered around the table. After a while I began to understand exactly how the process worked. The spirits that were taken to that group went through various kinds of therapies and treatments. The furious ones were given a chance to feel a presence of love while the desperate ones had their hopes rebuilt. Vibrations of care, kindness and protection surrounded the abandoned ones. The starving and thirsty souls were relieved of their torments. All of this happened under the guidance and in the name of Jesus Christ. Now I understand that only He and His example are the way, the truth and the light that guides our ignorant minds that still inhabit this planet of trials, challenges and atonements. He is the way that leads us all to a more illuminated path.

When I was better and my spiritual body was free from all the residue of the drugs, my conscience expanded. I was able to remember many details about my previous lives. I remembered my parents who are quite old today. Sometimes I visit them on Earth. I can already pray sincerely for them, and anxiously await the day where we will all reunite in the spiritual world. When that happens, we will begin to develop a new plan, for a renewed opportunity to coexist in the flesh. With God's permission, we shall help each other, by loving and forgiving one another, thanks to a deeper knowledge and understanding of the Gospel of Jesus.

CHAPTER 13

STARTING OVER - HOPE

I became a diligent student of the Gospel here in the spiritual world. In fact, I had already been a student in the distant past. I was a bishop in the 14th Century. Unfortunately, back then other interests fuelled my desire to study. I was compelled by my ambition to abandon the original path of righteousness I had chosen. I used all the knowledge to become rich and powerful so I could rule the town I lived in. I wanted the convenient lifestyle of a rich man who didn't need to work for a living. I had been given the gift of speech and was a brilliant orator, but my heart remained indifferent to Jesus. Now it's different. The presence of Christ is palpable to my senses. I now acknowledge that His mercy and compassion were manifested all around me. I was given the kindness of the rescuers who pulled me out of my nightmare and were beside me every step of the way, always patient, always with a smile. The words of Jesus were in my mind since the 14th Century. But today, they finally found their way into my heart.

And so I begin the amazing journey towards the Light. I'm no longer misguided by doubtful shortcuts or 'easy ways out'. My perseverance and good resolutions will be put to the test in a future lifetime, where I'll reunite with people from my past, in the physical world, both friends and enemies. We will then have the opportunity to settle our debts. I will reunite with my parents, who were my children in the 17th Century. During that existence, I had raised them in a wealthy and lavish environment filled with indifference and careless attitudes... As a result, their spirits did not fully absorb any meaningful lessons to take with them. But my previous debts do not stop there. I bring from my past the ability to manipulate situations and people to my benefit and their detriment. I used my intelligence and savvy business skills to foster ventures and take advantage of others, sometimes destroying families.

After walking through the dark path of the drugs, I feel like I'm starting 'from scratch'. I've asked permission from our superior brothers in the spiritual world to relate this story of my most recent lifetime on earth, hoping that parents, who read this, can become aware of the essential importance of raising their children under the light of the Gospel, from an early age. They will grow up with a strong foundation and reach adolescence with a safe and confident outlook for their future. Prayer is a powerful tool that protects us from the influences of evil and dark shortcuts. We all encounter or come across paths like these while in the physical world. Children need to be aware of the realities of eternal life and only a fresh, happy and positive view of Christ can captivate, enlighten and support our youth through their journey into adulthood. The resources for this strong foundation are composed of love, compassion, understanding, friendship and open dialogue between parents and their children.

Children are a divine treasure that we must protect and guide. By always relying on love, we help them remove the dust that they bring from previous journeys, so that their inner light may shine and their goodness be reflected upon all humanity. With this love, they remain fostered and cherished under the mantle of Jesus. He will protect them from robbers, corruptors and the wide doors that lead to tragedy.

Love one another, because only love covers the multitude of sin. Educate and instruct yourselves, because the knowledge of the Truth shall set you free.

André K.

Winterthur, Switzerland, October, 1995

NOTE:

This communication was received by the medium Gorete Newton during the month of October, 1995 in Winterthur, Switzerland.

EPILOGUE

MARCH 1, 2007

Today, 30 years after my departure from the physical world, I find myself in a new phase in my life. I have never been happier!

By dedicating my time to serving the greater good, I have been rebuilding the path for my future.

Being fully healed today, I now work in the recovery ward, helping recently deceased spirits who still struggle with their drug addictions.

The staff of workers from "Brotherly Love Home" and "Recovery Home" is almost totally comprised of discarnate entities whose physical deaths were caused by drug addictions and who have since been fully recovered, and are now helping those who arrive, brought in by the love and mercy of Jesus.

Since 1993, when the spiritual activities of these recovery wards began, all efforts were being directed towards the total elimination of the "Platzspitz" in the physical sphere. That place needed to urgently disappear. This sad meeting place of so many unloved and abandoned sons and daughters, mutually tied by the chains of addiction, was seen by society as a haven for renegades, when instead, it should have been seen as a place from which their own brothers and sisters were calling out to them, in desperate need of help.

The lights from the heavens brightened and shone down on Zurich, enlightening consciences, who were able to put an end to this huge problem, bleeding in the heart of their city. Since then, more dignity has been given to those who are still struggling with addictions.

Today we strive to prevent these terrible spectacles from resurfacing; horrid scenes which vividly expose misery to society, which in turn proceeds to quickly judge and condemn, like a senseless and unconscionable mob.

We also work hard to protect and inspire all those who rise to the service of consoling and guiding those brothers and sisters who find their lives controlled by drugs.

Help us with your prayers so that we can amass more spiritual resources needed for the successful completion of our tasks!

Andre K.

One day we shall see the Earth free from this cruel and devastating weapon, which disguises itself in the

illusions of unconscious fleeing, eventually destroy-
ing the dreams and aspirations of those who fall in its
trap.

Gorete Newton

Acknowledgements

I wish to dedicate this book to all those who died as a result of drug consumption and trafficking; to the sons and daughters of addicted parents, to the drug addicts of today, and to every youth in the world who may be tempted to consume drugs.

1995

When I began writing his story, I experienced every moment, while in trance, as if I was fully immersed in it. I would see, with my spiritual vision every detail.

At the time it was very difficult, since Andre was not yet fully recovered and it was emotionally painful for me to be mentally connected and vividly witnessing the situations and scenarios he was describing. I waited many years to mature and strengthen myself in orderto prepare for the likely events that may unfold as a result of this publication. In 1995 I did not speak German and until last year was under the impression that he had a different last name. It was only on March 1, 2007 that he took my hand and wrote his correct last name, which surprised me. In the interest of ethics, we shall not disclose his true identity.

TO PARENTS

It is not always us who are to blame for children who end up in the abyss of addictions. But it's up to us to observe our sons and daughters, to get to know them, educate and love them unconditionally; to impose limits, when necessary which will make them aware of our love, and as a result strengthen them to be protected from one of the biggest evils of our century: drugs

We have the duty to instruct our children about them. Many parents overlook this and do not even clarify their children, usually acting in an irresponsibly 'modern' attitude of accepting that their children should try what they want.

We have the duty to protect our children, but we cannot be blind to their flaws; we cannot assume for them the responsibility which they should take.

Let us listen to our children. Let us find out who they are, what they are suffering from, and how they feel about life. What are their dreams? What are their passions, their tendencies?

At meals, around the dinner table, we help form the future citizens of the world. It's not enough to be mothers and fathers; we need to be friends participating in their victories and failures, always ready to lift them up in the moments they fall, but never take the walk for them!

I know families that were destroyed as a result of having some of its members "socially" consume drugs.

Above all, let us be the example, so that our words are respected.

TO SONS AND DAUGHTERS

When you are going through periods of inner turmoil, family issues or emotional problems, look for help! Talk about your problems to someone who can understand. Seek a psychologist, a doctor, a friend, a parent, but don't try to solve the problem alone by running away towards paths that may have no return. Don't try to find comfort for what you're suffering in drugs, alcohol or anything like that.

Living with parents during adolescence has always been difficult. But do you revolt against them because they impose limits on you? Thank them and understand instead. Many of the young people that you see suffering, anguished or addicted, are children of carelessness and indifference. Their parents didn't care what they did, or would simply let them do whatever they wanted; giving them total freedom, and ignoring them in the process. Many times in order to enjoy their undeserved moments of rest, they would dump responsibilities on their children without them being physically or mentally ready; as a result, they planted seeds of hopelessness in their hearts, causing them to run away from their families and their own reality.

If you seek the discovery of unknown emotions, put yourselves on the good path and look around you! So many people need you! We can all be helpful. Dry up tears, hug a friend, overcome obstacles, conquer difficulties and tell others how you were able to make it; save lives!

The future is built by our efforts.

Think positively and make your dreams come true!

Dream, dream a lot, but be careful with ambition; it enslaves you and sucks out the joy of living from the soul.

Have realistic dreams, take risks, but responsibly!
And what if you fall? Stand up and start over until you learn to walk safely. Trust God, He will help you at every step of the journey!

Be strong when someone offers you something to 'get high on', or 'have a trip'.

Be strong when facing the arguments used by those who want you to become addicted. Don't believe them when they say that this or that drug is not harmful or addictive, it's a lie!

Some are able to get out of the sea of drugs without drowning, but many ruin their lives or they die slowly, vegetating while being numb from feeling the joy and beauty of life!

APPEAL TO DRUG DEALERS

I beg you, all who sell legal or illegal drugs: please, think of what you're doing for humanity. So much pain, so many deaths, so many lives destroyed or in the midst of being destroyed. You will also die one day. How will you be received by God? If your answer is "the devil is going to receive me." I have bad news for you. The devil does not exist!

It will be your own conscience that will make you suffer immensely on the other side of life, especially when the bitter fruits being planted today will have to be eaten by you or by those you love or will love one day. Life does not end with the death of the physical body! May God have mercy on all those who produce, sell or consume drugs.

"Each will be rewarded according to his works"*

One day we shall see the Earth free from this cruel and devastating weapon, which disguises itself in the illusions of unconscious fleeing, eventually destroying the dreams and aspirations of those who fall in its trap.

Gorete Newton,

August 5, 2007, Winterthur, Switzerland

"WITHOUT CHARITY THERE IS NO SALVATION"
ALLAN KARDEC

---

* MATTHEW 16:27

ABOUT THE MEDIUM

Gorete Newton is a native of Brazil, born on March 20, 1963 in the city of Cubatão in the state of São Paulo.

Her mediumship first surfaced in 1985, through the form of serious depression episodes and hallucinations.

Thanks to the eminent Spiritist medium and speaker Divaldo Pereira Franco, she was cured and her balance restored in less than 24 hours. Since then, she began studying Spiritism and the practice of mediumship.

She moved to Switzerland in 1992, joining a study group which later founded the first Spiritist Center in Zurich, where she was a volunteer director of philosophic studies, under the leadership of president Suzana da Silva Maia. She founded the first Spiritist Center in Winterthur, where she currently resides.

Since 1986, she has been a speaking medium* followed by psychography* in 1991, while living in Mexico City.

In 1995 she began receiving this small account from the spirit of Andre K, whose last incarnation took place in Zurich, Switzerland.

She's currently a directing member of the UCESS, The Swiss Union of Spiritst Centers, affiliated with the International Spiritist Council.

Gorete Newton is married to Udo Newton and has three children, Carolina, Viktor and Igor.

---

* *Speaking* medium or *Psychophonic* medium.
Pscychophony (from the Greek psyke, soul and phone, sound, voice) is the name given by Spiritism and some other spiritualist traditions to the phenomenon where a spirit talks using the voice of a medium. *(See The Mediums' Book by Allan Kardec)*

* *Psychography* is defined as a type of intelligent manifestation by Allan Kardec, where a spirit writes using the hand of a medium. Also known as "automatic writing". *(See The Spirits' Book by Allan Kardec)*

"To be born, to die,
to be reborn yet again
and progress, that is the law."

"All spirits are destined to perfection
and God gives them the means to
achieve it, through reincarnation."

HIPPOLYTE LÉON DENIZARD RIVAIL

(Allan Kardec) was born in Lyon, France, on October 3, 1804, in a traditional family, greatly distinguished in the legal profession and court system. He did not pursue those careers. From his youth, he was inclined toward the studies of science and philosophy.

Educated in the renowned School of Pestalozzi, in Yverdun (Switzerland), he became one of that celebrated teacher's most eminent pupils and one of the most zealous propagandists of the Educational system that exercised a great influence in the reform of the Educational system in France and in Germany.

Endowed with a notable intelligence, he was drawn to teaching, due to his character and his special aptitudes. At fourteen, he had already started to teach what he had previously studied, to some of his schoolmates, who had assimilated less than he. It was at that school that the ideas originated, which would later categorize him in the class of the progressive and free-thinkers individuals of the day.

To learn more about Spiritism, read the works of Allan Kardec:

- The Spirits' Book

- The Medium's Book

- The Gospel According To Spiritism

- Heaven and Hell

- Genesis

Spiritism around the World:

International Spiritist Council
www.spiritist.org

Spiritism in the U.S. :
www.usspiritistcouncil.com

Spiritism in the U.K.:
www.bussorg.co.uk

Spiritism in Switzerland
www.spiritismus.ch
www.ceeak.ch

Made in the USA
Charleston, SC
22 November 2009